A Guide for Using

Brown Bear, Brown Bear, What Do You See?

in the Classroom

Based on the book written by Bill Martin, Jr.

This guide written by Mary Bolte

Teacher Created Materials, Inc.
6421 Industry Way
Westminister, CA 92683
www.teachercreated.com
©1999 Teacher Created Materials, Inc.
Made in U.S.A.
ISBN-1-57690-625-6

Edited by
Leasha Taggart

Illustrated by
Agi Palinay
Jethro Wall

Cover Art by
Dennis Carmichael

Table of Contents

Introduction

"Brown Bear, Brown Bear, what do you see?" "I see millions of readers reading with me." This is what all beginning, fluent readers will experience in each Bill Martin, Jr., picture book included in this unit. His simple, repetitious, rhythmical, and skillful use of words will inspire and motivate readers to continue on to the unusual endings. Included in this variety of whimsical stories are more than a dozen picture books which will introduce young readers to the world of word decoding as they develop their reading skills through the use of word families, rhymes, and creative word usage. This unit is primarily concerned with two of Martin's bear books: *Brown Bear, Brown Bear, What Do You See?* and *Polar Bear, Polar Bear, What Do You Hear?* We hope you will include his other books and suggested activities in the Appendix, as young readers will become attached to his writing style. The generic work sheets on pages 39–42 can be used for a variety of independent writing and drawing activities.

A Sample Lesson Plan

The Sample Lesson Plan on page 4 provides you with a specific set of lesson plan suggestions. Each of the lessons can take from one to several days to complete and can include all or some of the suggested activities. Refer to the Suggestions for Using the Unit Activities on pages 7–11 for information relating to the unit activities.

A Unit Planner

If you wish to tailor the suggestions on pages 7–11 to a format other than the one prescribed in the Sample Lesson Plan, a blank Unit Planner is provided on page 5. On a specific day you may choose the activities that you wish to include by writing the activity number or a brief notation about the lesson in the Unit Activities section. Space has been provided for reminders, comments, and other pertinent information related to each day's activities. Reproduce copies of the Unit Planner as needed.

Sample Lesson Plan

Lesson 1

- Read Getting to Know the Book and the Author (page 6) with your students.
- Do Before the Book activities 2, 4, 5, and 6 on page 7.
- Read the story for enjoyment.

Lesson 2

- Introduce the vocabulary on page 7.
- Reread the story, listening for the vocabulary words.
- Retell the story, using the What Did Brown Bear See? activity on page 19.
- Complete A Dozen Bear Words activity on page 20.
- Complete The Bear Parade activity on page 27.
- Explore the continents, using the Bears Around the World activity on page 33.

Lesson 3

- Complete The Panda Bear: A Bear or a Raccoon? activity on page 21.
- Continue the panda bear inquiry with the Now, What Is Your Opinion? activity on page 22.
- Discover the origin of the teddy bear, using the Theodore and Teddy activity on page 34.
- Continue the teddy bear inquiry with the Teddy and Theodore activity on page 35.

Lesson 4

- Learn about different groups of animals living on land or water with the Where Do Animals Live? activity on page 36.
- Read *Polar Bear, Polar Bear, What Do You Hear?* and complete the two graphing activities, Let's Graph the Bear's Animal Friends and Let's Graph the Animals on pages 28 and 29.
- Investigate adjectives and nouns using the What Did Polar Bear See? activity on page 24.
- In groups, write songs for Martin's two bear stories. Refer to the Ant, Ant, What Do You Hear? activity on page 32.

Lesson 5

- Work in groups to make stick puppet theaters and stick puppets on pages 16–18. In addition, students can make their own child stick puppets.
- As a class Create a Reader's Theater Script, page 43.
- Complete the rebus story activity, Tracks in the Snow on page 23.
- Explore the similarities and differences between animals and humans, using the Comparing Animals and Humans activity on page 37.
- Discover the vibrant colors and collage style used to illustrate the book, using the Colorful Animal Collage activity on page 38.
- Practice problem-solving skills, using the Solve Zooka Zookeeper's Problem on page 30.

Lesson 6

- Learn about the five senses and create a poem using the poem on page 31 as a model.
- Write your own sense poem, using the format of the My Senses Poem activity on page 26 or Paw Prints on page 41.
- Present the reader's theater script, the various ant songs, and the sense poems to a live audience.

Unit Planner

Unit Activities		Unit Activities	
(Date)		(Date)	
Notes/Comments:		Notes/Comments:	
Unit Activities		Unit Activities	
(Date)		(Date)	
Notes/Comments:		Notes/Comments:	
Unit Activities		Unit Activities	
(Date)		(Date)	
Notes/Comments:		Notes/Comments:	

Getting to Know the Book and the Author

About the Book

Brown Bear, Brown Bear, What Do You See? is published by Henry Holt and Company, New York. *(Available in Canada, Fitz Henry Whiteside; UK, PanDemic Limited; AUS, CIS Publishers)*

What does a loving mother really see in this book? A brown bear? A white dog? Beautiful children? What do beautiful children really see in this book? A brown bear? A purple cat? A loving mother looking at them?

They all see each other, plus a brown bear who initiates a tale and introduces colorful Eric Carle collages as the readers become absorbed with the sounds of words in rhyme. The progressive use of primary and secondary colors (plus gold) helps to dramatize the images as Bill Martin, Jr. and Eric Carle collaborate to create an astounding book that will motivate readers to enjoy reading. As you use this Literature Unit, remember the author's advice: "Educators need to resume the role of student in order to progress . . . as better students become better teachers."

About the Author

Bill Martin, Jr. is a literature icon of the 20th century! Reading was a lifelong priority and challenge in Bill Martin, Jr.'s life. As a young child in Kansas in the early 1900s, William Ivan Martin experienced difficulty in learning to read, which followed him throughout high school and college.

As a young boy Martin learned to depend upon his ears to relate sounds to the printed word. His fifth-grade teacher read aloud to the class daily and was a positive influence on his future. In high school, an influential drama teacher exposed Martin to Shakespeare and drama. He soon realized that the spoken word was a priority in his life. Without taking a reading test, he was enrolled in Kansas State Teachers College, now Emporia State University. As a freshman, he was inspired when he finally completed the reading of an entire book in a composition class. Upon graduation, he became a high school English, drama, and journalism teacher in Kansas. When World War II entered Martin's life, he became a newspaper editor for the U.S. Air Force. During this time he wrote his first book, *The Little Squeegy Bug*, illustrated by his brother Bernard. This duo continued to collaborate on children's books.

In the mid-fifties and early sixties, Martin attended graduate school in education at Northeastern University and also became the principal at Crow Island Elementary School in Winnetka, Illinois. Publishing became Martin's next challenge as he joined Holt, Rinehart and Winston as a creator of elementary classroom materials. His innovative programs related printed words to sounds and encouraged the use of word clusters which could be sung together to develop meaning. In the late sixties, Martin left the publishing business and pursued an editing and freelance writing career, which resulted in the publication of over 200 books for children.

Suggestions for Using the Unit Activities

Use some or all of the following suggestions to introduce your students to *Brown Bear, Brown Bear, What Do You See?* and to extend their appreciation of the book through activities that cross the curriculum. The suggested activities have been divided into three sections to assist you in planning the literature unit.

The suggestions are in the following sections:

- *Before the Book:* includes suggestions for preparing the classroom environment and the students for the literature to be read.
- *Into the Book:* has activities that focus on the book's contents, characters, themes, etc.
- *After the Book:* extends the readers' enjoyment of the book.

Before the Book

1. Before you begin the unit, prepare the vocabulary cards, story questions, and sentence strips for the pocket chart activities. (See the Into the Book section and page 15.)
2. Discuss bears and brainstorm different kinds of bears, including real and imaginary ones.
3. Read about Bill Martin, Jr., on page 6.
4. Set the stage for reading the book by discussing the following questions: What is a bear? What do you think Brown Bear will see in the book? Where do you think Brown Bear is? Where do bears live?
5. Display the cover of the book. Ask questions about the cover, such as: What do you see on the cover? What do you think the bear is looking at? Where do you think the bear is? Have you ever seen a real bear? What colors do you see on the cover? How did Eric Carle design this bear? What is a collage? Have you ever made a collage?
6. Review the eight basic colors using crayons, markers, etc., and discuss animals that could be these colors.

Into the Book

1. Pocket Chart Activities: Vocabulary Words

After reading the book, discuss the meanings of the following sets of words in context. Make copies of the bear on page 14 on different colors of paper. Write each set of words on the bears. Display the bears in a pocket chart. (See page 12.)

brown bear	yellow duck
purple cat	black sheep
red bird	blue horse
white dog	green frog

Suggestions for Using the Unit Activities *(cont.)*

Into the Book *(cont.)*

2. Pocket Chart Activities: Story Questions

Develop critical thinking skills, using the Story Questions on page 15. The questions are based upon Bloom's Taxonomy and are provided for each level of Bloom's Levels of Learning. Reproduce the bear pattern on page 14. Write each question on a bear and place it on a pocket chart.

3. More Pocket Chart Activities

- Draw animals on the bear pattern (page 14) in the order in which they appeared in the story.
- Write descriptive riddles about each animal on sentence strips. Display the riddles in the pocket chart for students to solve.
- Brainstorm a list of sentences retelling the story. Display them in the pocket chart.
- Write each question in the story on a sentence strip. Then display the questions in the pocket chart for the students to answer.

4. Language Arts

- *What Did Brown Bear See? (page 19)*

  Read the directions and discuss the Colors and Animals word lists. Independently or together, match the colors to the animals as they appear in the book. Then complete the pictures.

- *A Dozen Bear Words (page 20)*

  Discuss the directions. Read the story together, emphasizing each underlined word and its meaning. Have students complete the word search independently. The words can go horizontally, vertically, diagonally, and backwards.

- *The Panda Bear: A Bear or a Raccoon? (page 21)*

  Display pictures of the giant panda bear and the red panda bear. Do research on the two animals and discuss their physical characteristics. Read the story and then follow the directions.

- *Now, What Is Your Opinion? (page 22)*

  After reading The Panda Bear: A Bear or a Raccoon? on page 21 and discussing the two animals, have students write about their opinions in answer to the following question: Is a panda bear a raccoon or a bear?

- *Tracks in the Snow (page 23)*

  Discuss rebus stories and how they are written (with the use of pictures instead of words). Discuss the footprints and how footprints are made. Think of wet or dry ways that students can make their own footprints. Then complete the activity together or independently.

Suggestions for Using the Unit Activities *(cont.)*

Into the Book *(cont.)*

4. Language Arts *(cont.)*

- *What Did Polar Bear See?* *(page 24)*

  Discuss the meanings of adjectives and nouns. Then read *Polar Bear, Polar Bear, What Do You Hear?*, and point out how the author used adjectives and nouns in the story. Complete the activity together or independently.

- *A Circle Poem* *(page 25)*

  Read *Listen to the Rain*. (See page 46.) Discuss the meanings of the adjectives and list the adjectives in the book. Together, choose a theme and brainstorm words to describe the theme. Then read and follow the directions in this activity.

- *My Senses Poem* *(page 26)*

  Discuss the five senses: hearing, sight, smell, taste, and touch. Write your own poem using the My Poem of Senses outline. (See page 31 for ideas.) This poem can be written on a copy of the lined Paw Prints on page 41.

5. Math

- *The Bear Parade* *(page 27)*

  Provide each student with a strip of paper 6" x 36" (15 cm x 91 cm) or longer. Make copies of the four bears on white paper. Emphasize the differences among the four bears. Read and follow directions. Share and discuss the different parade patterns.

- *Let's Graph the Bear's Animal Friends* and *Let's Graph the Animals!* *(pages 28 and 29)*

  After reading *Brown Bear, Brown Bear, What Do You See?* and *Polar Bear, Polar Bear, What Do You Hear?*, discuss these animal groups: amphibians, birds, fish, insects, mammals, and reptiles. Then slowly reread the book and complete page 28. When finished with page 28, complete the graph on page 29 to determine how many animals were in each group. Create word problems and questions about the graph.

- *Solve Zooka Zookeeper's Problem* *(page 30)*

  Discuss different animals and their number of legs, emphasizing combinations of twos and fours. Read and follow the directions for each zoo gate.

6. Health

- *Making Sense of Our Senses* *(page 31)*

  Discuss the five senses: hearing, sight, smell, taste, and touch. Brainstorm examples of each of the senses and how we use them each day. Read the poem together. Then have students write their own sense poems on a copy of the form on page 41.

Suggestions for Using the Unit
Activities *(cont.)*

Into the Book *(cont.)*

7. Music

- *Ant, Ant, What Do You Hear?* *(page 32)*

  Sing this song to the tune of "Frére Jacques." In groups of five, students add their names to the "Ant" song. Practice the song and present it to an audience. Original stick puppets can be made to accompany the song.

8. Social Studies

- *Bears Around the World* *(page 33)*

  Locate the seven continents on a world map. Research why no wild bears live in Africa, Antarctica, and Australia. Discuss the directions and complete the activity independently.

- *Theodore and Teddy* *(page 34)*

  Read the story about President Theodore Roosevelt. Share times when you have helped someone. Discuss the four parts of a story. Then follow directions and write the story on the lined Paw Prints on page 41.

- *Teddy and Theodore* *(page 35)*

  Discuss and share teddy bear stories. Ask students to tell about their teddy bears. Display pictures of different kinds of teddy bears or have a Teddy Bear Day. Read the story and define the words "plush" and "excelsior." Complete the remainder of the activity.

9. Science

- *Where Do Animals Live?* *(page 36)*

  Review the five groups of animals named on page 29. Brainstorm and list examples for each group. Use various methods to research and learn more about their characteristics. Then discuss where these animals live and complete the lesson.

- *Comparing Animals and Humans* *(page 37)*

  Discuss ways in which humans and animals are alike. Use the lined Paw Prints (page 41) to list these characteristics. Then complete this activity by writing about how humans and animals are different.

10. Art

- *Colorful Animal Collage* *(page 38)*

  Discuss the way the illustrator Eric Carle uses vibrant colors and a collage method to create his illustrations. Then complete the activity to make individual collages. Use these to make a large, class collage.

Suggestions for Using the Unit Activities *(cont.)*

Into the Book *(cont.)*

11. Generic Activities

- *Word Families (page 39)*

  Thirty-seven word families account for at least 500 words. These include *ack, ail, ain, ake, ale, ame, an, ank, ap, ash, at, ate, aw, ay, eat, ell, est, ice, ick, ide, ight, ill, in, ine, ing, ink, ip, it, ock, oke, op, ore, ot, uck, ug, ump* and *unk*. Choose two of these at a time and brainstorm words with similar word endings. Write rhymes using these words.

- *A Celebration (page 40)*

  This activity can be used with *The Happy Hippopotami* or as a supplemental activity for another Bill Martin, Jr. book.

- *Paw Prints (pages 41 and 42)*

  Use the lined copy for writing rhymes, poetry, stories, etc., relating to the unit activities. The unlined copy can be used for illustrative purposes, etc.

After the Book

Culminating Activity

Have a class Bill Martin, Jr., Rhyme Revue, presenting drama, music, and poetry.

1. Drama

- *Create a Reader's Theater Script (page 43)*

  Develop a script as a class to be performed in the reader's theater style. Provide a copy of the script for each performer. Highlight the parts and laminate the scripts before distributing them. In groups, students can choose or be assigned parts. Practice reading the script together, using the stick puppets on pages 17 and 18. When performing, the performers can stand in a line or in a semicircle. As each part is read, the reader holds up the stick puppet.

2. Music

Sing "Ant, Ant, What Do You Hear?" on page 32, using the words the children wrote. Create original stick puppets, masks, or decorative name tags to identify each character.

3. Poetry

Read the sense poems from page 26 created by the students. A visual aid could be displayed as each poem is read. Divide a 12" x 18" (30 cm x 46 cm) piece of construction paper into six equal parts. Write the poem's title in the first section. Then draw an illustration to match each "sense verse" in the poem.

Pocket Chart Activities

Prepare a pocket chart for storing and using vocabulary cards, the question cards, and the sentence strips.

How to Make a Pocket Chart

If a commercial pocket chart is unavailable, you can make a pocket chart if you have access to a laminator. Begin by laminating a 24" x 36" (61 cm x 91 cm) piece of colored tagboard. Run about 20" (51 cm) of additional plastic. To make nine pockets, cut the clear plastic into nine equal strips. Space the strips equally down the 36" (91 cm) length of the tagboard. Attach each strip with cellophane tape along the sides and bottom. This will hold the sentence strips, word cards, etc., and can be displayed in a learning center or mounted on a chalk rail for use with a group. When your pocket chart is ready, use it to display sentence strips, vocabulary words, and question cards. A sample chart is provided below.

How to Use a Pocket Chart

1. On brown, light brown, or tan paper, reproduce the bear pattern on page 14. Make vocabulary cards as directed on page 7. Print the definitions on sentence strips for a matching activity.
2. Write the questions in the book on separate sentence strips. Match the vocabulary words as the correct answers.
3. Display the question sentence strips in order as they appear in the book.

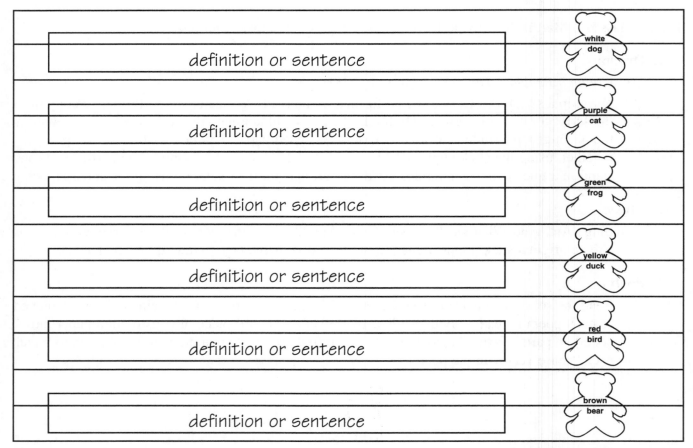

Story Questions

Use the following questions for the suggested activities on page 13. Prepare the bear pattern (page 14) and write a different question on each bear.

I. KNOWLEDGE (*ability to recall learned information*)
- Who is Brown Bear?
- Who do the goldfish see?
- What do the children see looking at them?
- What does the mother see looking at her?

II. COMPREHENSION (*ability to master basic understanding of information*)
- What are the colors of the different animals?
- What are the two rhyming words used throughout the book? How are they used?
- When does the reader really discover who is looking at the animals?

III. APPLICATION (*ability to do something new with information*)
- Where do you think the children are when they see the animals?
- Why is the mother looking at the children, and whose mother is she?
- How do the children resemble the animals looking at them?
- Why do you think the author had nine animals and nine children in the book?

IV. ANALYSIS (*ability to examine the parts of a whole*)
- Why are the children looking at the animals?
- When in the story do you realize the animals are looking at the children?
- How does Eric Carle, the illustrator, help to develop the story in the book?

V. SYNTHESIS (*ability to bring together information to make something new*)
- What do you think will happen after the mother, children, and animals are finished looking at each other?
- There are nine children and nine animals in the book. How would you write a new ending for the story?
- What would you think of the story if all the animals looked alike and all the children looked alike?

VI. EVALUATION (*ability to form and defend an opinion*)
- Do you think the children enjoy looking at the animals? Why or why not?
- Do you think the animals enjoy looking at the children? Why or why not?
- Does this story have a surprise ending? Why do you think so?

Stick Puppet Theaters

Make a class set of puppet theaters (one for each student) or make one theater for every two to four students. The patterns and directions for making the stick puppets are on pages 17 and 18.

Materials

- 22" x 28" (56 cm x 71 cm) pieces of colored poster board (enough for each student or group of students)
- markers, crayons, or paints
- scissors or a craft knife

Directions

1. Fold the poster board 8" (20 cm) in front of the shorter sides. (See picture below.)
2. Cut a window in the front panel, large enough to accommodate two or three stick puppets.
3. Let the children personalize and decorate their own theaters.
4. Laminate the stick puppet theaters to make them more durable. You may wish to send the theaters home at the end of the year, or save them to use year after year.

Suggestions for Using the Puppets and the Puppet Theaters

1. Prepare the stick puppets, using the directions on page 17. Use the puppets and the puppet theaters with the reader's theater script developed from page 43. Students will create their own "children" stick puppets.
2. Students can make their own stick puppets to correspond with *Brown Bear, Brown Bear, What Do You See?* or *Polar Bear, Polar Bear, What Do You Hear?* Then let them retell the stories, using their own words or by reading from the book.
3. Read questions from the book, and ask the students to hold up the stick puppets to answer the questions.

Stick Puppet Patterns

Directions: Reproduce the patterns on tagboard or construction paper. Have the students color the patterns. Cut them along the dashed lines. To complete the stick puppets, glue each pattern to a tongue depressor or craft stick. Use the stick puppets with puppet theaters, the ant songs, the sense poems, and/or the reader's theater script.

Stick Puppet Patterns *(cont.)*

See page 17 for directions.

What Did Brown Bear See?

When Brown Bear sees an animal, he describes it by using a color word. Read the book again, and match the colors to the animals.

Colors	Animals
black	frog
green	duck
gold	horse
yellow	cat
white	sheep
blue	bird
brown	fish
red	dog
purple	bear

Choose three of the colors and then draw and color something that is each of those colors. Write the name of the item on the bottom line.

_____	_____	_____

A Dozen Bear Words

Read the story about bears. Find the word "bear" and the other underlined bear words in the word search below.

There are many different kinds of bears. Some are called <u>brown</u> bears, <u>grizzly</u> bears, <u>black</u> bears and <u>polar</u> bears. <u>Teddy</u> bears are favorites of children. A <u>bear</u> is a <u>carnivore</u>, which means it eats mostly meat. Bears use their <u>claws</u> to <u>hunt</u> for their food. Sometimes bears <u>hibernate</u> (sleep) in a cave during the winter. A baby bear is called a <u>cub</u> and is born with no fur. A cub grows <u>fur</u> after it is a month old and stays with its mother for one or two years until it has learned to hunt for food.

G	Z	I	B	Q	F	U	R	E
R	C	K	B	L	C	L	R	T
I	S	P	R	G	A	O	T	A
Z	Y	O	O	P	V	C	X	N
Z	M	L	W	I	E	Y	K	R
L	B	A	N	V	D	H	D	E
Y	E	R	J	D	N	C	U	B
W	A	F	E	H	U	N	T	I
C	R	T	C	L	A	W	S	H

The Panda Bear: A Bear or a Raccoon?

There are two kinds of pandas, the giant panda and the red panda. They both live in the mountains of China, eat bamboo, and climb trees.

The giant panda is black and white. Its legs, shoulders, ears, and eyes are black. The rest of its fur is white. It can be between five and six feet (1.5m–1.8m) long.

The red panda has a red coat, a white-striped face, and a bushy, ringed tail. It is about three feet long (91 cm), including the tail.

Color the pandas and then label them giant panda or red panda.

Now, What Is Your Opinion?

Now it's your turn to answer the question: "Are pandas bears or raccoons?" Tell why you the think the giant panda and the red panda could be bears or raccoons.

_____

_____

_____

_____

_____

_____

Draw a bear in one box and a raccoon in the other box. Label each picture on the line.

Tracks in the Snow

Have you ever seen animals' footprints in the snow, sand, or dirt? Read the rebus story and write the names of the animals and other pictures on the lines.

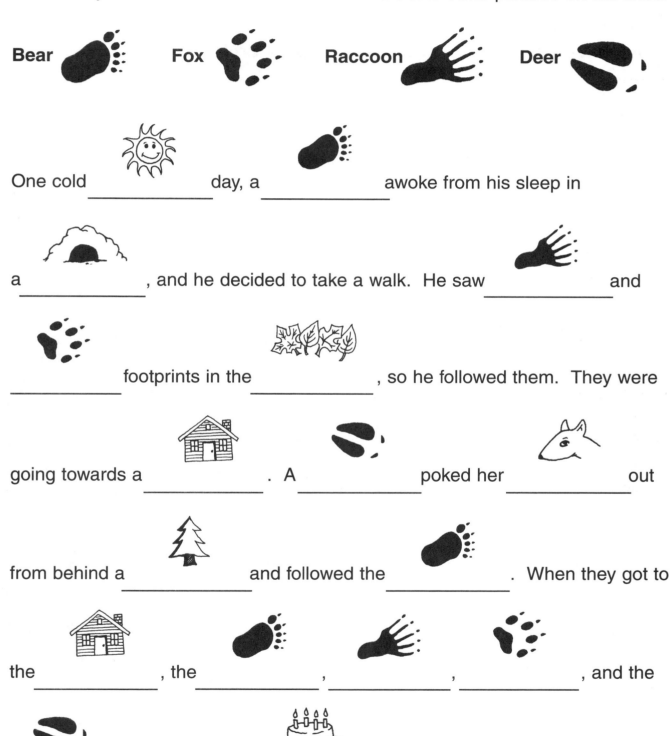

One cold _____ day, a _____ awoke from his sleep in

a _____ , and he decided to take a walk. He saw _____ and

_____ footprints in the _____ , so he followed them. They were

going towards a _____ . A _____ poked her _____ out

from behind a _____ and followed the _____ . When they got to

the _____ , the _____ , _____ , _____ , and the

_____ had a surprise _____ party for themselves.

What Did Polar Bear See?

Brown Bear used the word **purple** to describe the cat. Purple is an adjective.
An **adjective** describes a **noun**, (the name of a person, place or thing) like **cat**.

Noun = name of a person, place, or thing (Example: **cat**)

Adjective = a word that describes (Example: **Purple** cat)

- Write five **adjectives** inside the brown bear.

- Write five **nouns** inside the polar bear.

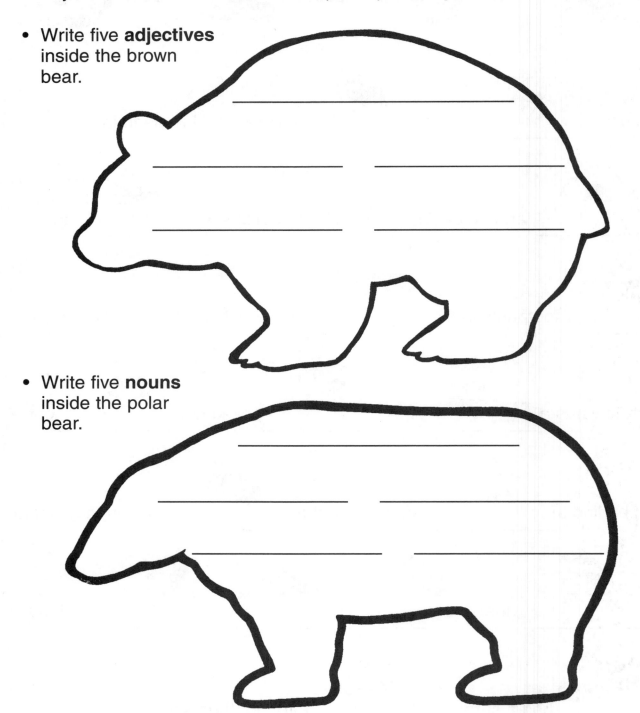

A Circle Poem

A circle poem is a poem that begins and ends the same way. Use nouns and adjectives to complete this circle poem.

An ***adjective*** is a word that describes a ***noun***. A ***noun*** is the name of a person, place, or thing.

Pretend to listen to something and write about it, using ***adjectives*** and ***nouns***.

_____
Title

1. Listen to the _____,
noun

2. The _____ _____,
adjective   *noun*

3. The _____, _____ _____.
adjective   *adjective*   *noun*

4. The _____ _____,
adjective   *noun*

5. Listen to the _____.
noun

My Senses Poem

Write your own poem of senses, using Teddy Bear's outline below.

My Poem of Senses

_____, _____,
what do you hear?

I hear _____,

_____.

_____, _____,
what do you see?

I see _____,

_____.

_____, _____,
what do you smell?

I smell _____,

_____.

_____, _____,
what do you taste?

I taste _____,

_____.

_____, _____,
what do you touch?

I touch _____,

_____.

The Bear Parade

The bears are having a parade but need to be in a special order. Color and cut out the bears and make a pattern to show their order in the parade. Then glue the bears to a strip of paper.

Brown Bear	Brown Bear	Brown Bear	Brown Bear
Black Bear	Black Bear	Black Bear	Black Bear
Polar Bear	Polar Bear	Polar Bear	Polar Bear
Teddy Bear	Teddy Bear	Teddy Bear	Teddy Bear

Let's Graph the Bear's Animal Friends

List the different animals in the *Brown Bear, Brown Bear, What Do You See?* and *Polar Bear, Polar Bear, What Do You Hear?* Next to each animal, write whether it is an amphibian, bird, fish, insect, mammal, or reptile. When you are finished with the list, complete the two graphs on the next page.

Brown Bear, Brown Bear. . .

1. ___brown bear___ ___mammal___
2. _____ _____
3. _____ _____
4. _____ _____
5. _____ _____
6. _____ _____
7. _____ _____
8. _____ _____
9. _____ _____

Polar Bear, Polar Bear. . .

1. ___polar bear___ ___mammal___
2. _____ _____
3. _____ _____
4. _____ _____
5. _____ _____
6. _____ _____
7. _____ _____
8. _____ _____
9. _____ _____

Let's Graph the Animals

Brown Bear's friends saw many different animals. Polar Bear's friends heard many different animals. Use your two lists from page 28 to graph the animals' groups on the graphs below.

Brown Bear, Brown Bear, What Do You See?

amphibian						
bird						
fish						
insect						
mammal						
reptile						

Polar Bear, Polar Bear, What Do You Hear?

amphibian						
bird						
fish						
insect						
mammal						
reptile						

Solve Zooka Zookeeper's Problem

One day the animals in the zoo got loose, and Zooka Zookeeper had to find them. She saw 12 legs behind the zoo's front gate.

Draw the legs of the other animals you think are hiding behind the gate. Write their names on the back of this paper.

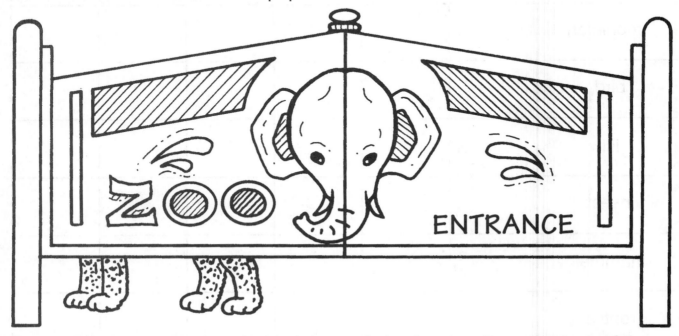

Then she saw 10 more legs behind the zoo's back gate. Draw the legs of the zoo animals that may be hiding there. Write their names on the back of this paper.

Making Sense of Our Senses

Bears, like humans, have senses: the senses of hearing, sight, smell, taste, and touch. Bears cannot hear or see very well. Read Teddy Bear's poem, and then write your own sense poem, using the same format.

Polar Bear, Polar Bear,
What do you hear?
I hear an icy noise,
And it is very near.

Panda Bear, Panda Bear,
What do you see?
I see a shadow,
And it's beside the tree.

Grizzly Bear, Grizzly Bear,
What do you smell?
I smell a skunk,
With his nose inside a shell.

Black Bear, Black Bear,
What do you taste?
I taste the flavor,
Of Italian tomato paste.

Teddy Bear, Teddy Bear,
What can you touch?
I can touch a child,
Who I love very much.

Ant, Ant, What Do You Hear?

Add your friends' names to this song. Then sing the song to the tune of "Frére Jacques" or "Are You Sleeping?"

_____ Ant, _____ Ant,

What do you hear? What do you hear?

I hear _____ Cricket, I hear _____ Cricket,

Chirping at me, Chirping at me.

_____ Cricket, _____ Cricket,

What do you hear? What do you hear?

I hear _____ Robin, I hear _____ Robin,

Tweeting at me, Tweeting at me.

_____ Robin, _____ Robin,

What do you hear? What do you hear?

I hear _____ Cat, I hear _____ Cat,

Meowing at me, Meowing at me.

_____ Cat, _____ Cat,

What do you hear? What do you hear?

I hear _____ Dog, I hear _____ Dog,

Barking at me, Barking at me.

_____ Dog, _____ Dog,

What do you hear? What do you hear?

I hear _____ and _____,

I hear _____ and _____,

Calling to me, calling to me.

_____, and _____, and _____,

_____, and _____, and _____,

What do you hear? What do you hear?

We hear all our friends. We hear all our friends.

Saying "We're great!" Saying "We're great!"

Bears Around the World

On Earth, there are seven continents: Africa, Asia, Australia, Antarctica, Europe, North America, and South America. Bears live on the continents of Asia, Europe, North America, and South America. No bears live on the continents of Africa, Antarctica, or Australia.

On the map below, draw bear faces on the four continents where bears live.

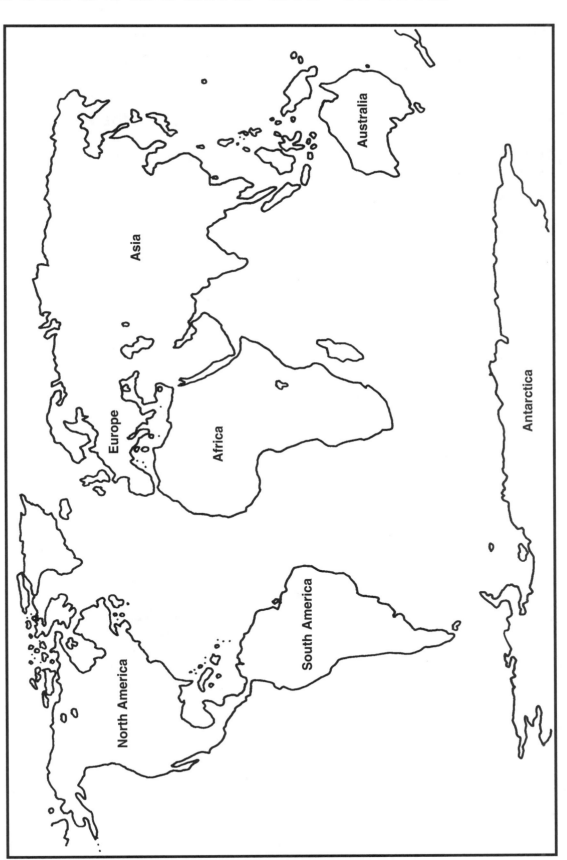

Theodore and Teddy

The teddy bear was born in Brooklyn, New York, in 1902 as a result of an event in the history of the United States. President Theodore Roosevelt was in Mississippi on a hunting trip with his friends. His friends captured a small, black bear and tied it to a tree. President Roosevelt refused to shoot the tired, little bear. He said it was not sportsmanlike so they set the bear free.

Write a story about a time that you helped an animal or someone else. Be sure to include the setting, the characters, the problem, and how you solved the problem.

Use the space below to plan your story.

Title_____

Setting	Characters
Problem	**Solution**

Teddy and Theodore

A few days after President Roosevelt saved the little black bear, Michael Michtom put two toy bears in his shop's window in Brooklyn, New York. His wife, Rose, had made them from plush and excelsior. They had brown, shoe-button eyes. Michael got permission from President Roosevelt to call them teddy bears. Since then, teddy bears have been loved and have become popular toys.

Every teddy bear should have a special name, just like you. Draw your own teddy bear in the window and then write your bear's name on the door. Write why it is so special on the lines below the box.

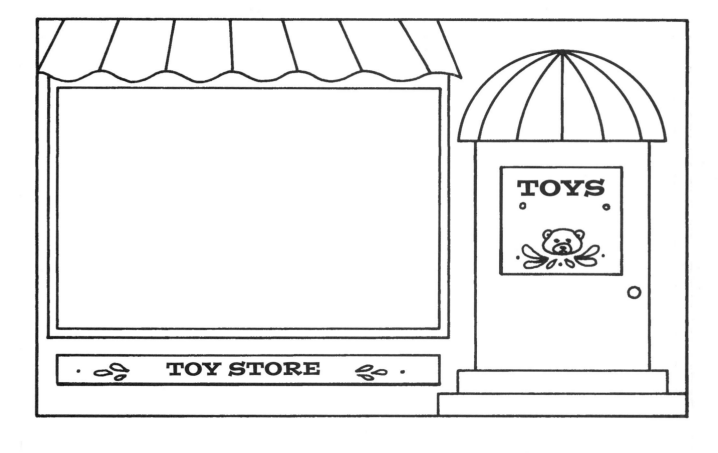

_____

_____

_____

Where Do Animals Live?

Below are five of the six groups of animals listed on page 29: amphibians, fish, insects, mammals, and reptiles.

Amphibians can live on land or in the water.
Fish spend their lives in water.
Insects spend their lives in water or on land.
Mammals mostly live on land, but some can live in water.
Reptiles live on land and in water.

Find pictures of each group of animals. Use the pictures to help you draw an example of each group of animals in the boxes below.

Amphibian	Fish
Insect	Mammal
Reptile	

Comparing Animals and Humans

Humans and animals are both living beings that can move by themselves, can get energy from the food they eat, can breathe, and can grow.

These are some ways that animals and humans are alike. Think of some ways that they are **different**. Write these ideas below.

Colorful Animal Collage

In both *Brown Bear, Brown Bear, What Do You See?* and *Polar Bear, Polar Bear, What Do You Hear?*, Eric Carle, the illustrator, creates vibrant pictures through the use of collages. Follow the directions below to create your own classroom collages.

Materials

- construction paper (various colors)
- paint
- crayons
- markers
- scissors
- glue
- any of the following: sandpaper, feathers, tree bark, wire screen, or any other textured items

Directions

- Begin by showing students the pictures from both books. Discuss the way varying shades of the same color are used in each picture. Also point out the differences in texture in the pictures.
- Allow each student time to choose an animal he or she would like to create. Before you pass out the paper, ask students to tell you their animals and then give them three sheets of 6" x 9" (15 cm x 23 cm) white construction paper. Also give each student a piece of construction paper in the color of the animal he or she has chosen.
- On each of the three pieces of white paper, the student is to use a different medium. For example, color one piece with a brown marker, paint one piece with brown paint, and put a piece of metal screen beneath the third piece and do a crayon rubbing. Along with the brown construction paper, the student now has four different shades and textures of brown paper.
- Using the four pieces of paper, students then each cut out the various parts of the animal and glue them onto a piece of white 9" x 12" (23 cm x 30 cm) construction paper.

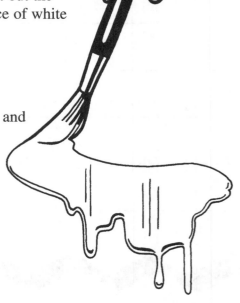

Additional Ideas

- Use collages to make a class book.
- Cut out the collages, glue craft sticks to the bottoms, and use them for the reader's theater (page 43).
- Cut out the collages and use them to create a class collage bulletin board.

Word Families

Write one word family on line 1 and another on line 2. Then think of words that have the same endings.

1. _____

_____

_____

_____

_____

_____

_____

_____

2. _____

_____

_____

_____

_____

_____

_____

_____

Now write two rhymes using the words in list 1 and list 2.

_____

_____

A Celebration

The Happy Hippopotami celebrated a holiday in May by going to the beach and having a party. Now it's your turn to plan a party or a celebration. Use the outline below to plan your party or celebration.

Who will come to the party?

_____

_____

What will we celebrate?

_____

_____

Why are we having a party?

_____

_____

Where will the party be?

_____

_____

When will we have the party?

_____

_____

Paw Prints

Paw Prints *(cont.)*

Create a Reader's Theater Script

Reader's theater is an exciting and easy method of providing students with the opportunity to perform a play while minimizing the use of props, sets, costumes, or memorization. Students read the dialogue of the characters or narrator from the book or a prepared script. The dialogue may be read from the book just as the author has written it, or the teacher and students may create a new script.

How to Create a Script

- Read through the book again with the students. Discuss the word pattern followed throughout the book.

- On pages 17 and 18, seven animal characters have been provided for you to use with the puppet theater. These may be used with the script, or new characters may be chosen.

- If new characters are chosen, ask students to suggest seven or eight characters to star in the play. Write their responses on the board or on a large piece of paper.

- Write on the board one example of the word pattern used in the book.

- Ask a student to choose one of the new characters, and insert the name into the word pattern.

- Continue with all of the characters until the script is complete.

- Copy the new script so that each student has a copy.

- Encourage students to use sound effects and dramatic voices while reading the play.

How to Make Simple Costumes

Although costumes are not necessary in a reader's theater production, your students may wish to wear simple costumes. Here are some suggestions:

- The students can wear signs around their necks, indicating their speaking parts. Prepare signs by writing the reader's character on a piece of construction paper. Staple a necklace-length piece of yarn to the top of the paper.

- The students may wear colored shirts to represent the colors of their animals in the play.

- Masks may be made out of paper plates. Give each student a paper plate. Either cut holes for their eyes and mouths ahead of time, or help them to do this before they start. Then provide students with paint, markers, or crayons to color their mask. Also provide yarn, felt, feathers, ribbon, or fabric for the students to further decorate their masks. Staple a piece of yarn across the back of each mask to help it stay on the student's head, or glue a craft stick to the bottom of the mask so it can be held in front of the student's face.

- Ears, antennae, and tails can also be made out of paper plates, yarn, fabric, pipe cleaners, or felt.

In a reader's theater production, everyone can be involved in some way. Encourage class members to participate in off-stage activities, such as greeting the audience and assisting behind the scenes.

Activities for Other Bill Martin, Jr. Books

A Beautiful Feast for a Big King Cat

Authors: Bill Martin, Jr. and John Archambault
Illustrator: Bruce Degan
Publisher: HarperCollins, 1994

1. Create an interactive reading experience. Have one group read the storyteller's lines and have another group read the italicized lines of Tiny Mouse, Mother Mouse, and Cat.

2. Write a reader's theater script using this rhyming story. Create parts for the characters: Cat, Tiny Mouse, Mother Mouse, and two or three narrators. In groups, practice the script and then perform it for a live audience.

3. Discuss and share a time when you tried to trick someone or when someone tried to trick you.

4. Discuss the word "bully" and use adjectives to describe a bully. Then create a list of opposites for these words, such a mean-kind, big-little, loud-quiet, etc.

5. List and categorize rhyming words in the story. Then add other new words to the lists with the same word endings.

6. Discuss how the mouse learned his lesson. Write a story about how you learned a lesson.

7. List your favorite foods. Then list the foods that Mouse wanted to serve Cat. How are the foods alike or different?

Barn Dance!

Authors: Bill Martin, Jr. and John Archambault
Illustrator: Ted Rand
Publisher: Henry Holt and Co., 1986

1. Read the book aloud to the students. Then echo-read the book again (you read and students repeat) with a rap beat.

2. List and discuss the different wild and domestic farm and rural animals featured in the book.

3. The animals danced with partners. Count by twos to match each student with a partner. If there is an odd number, match the student (skinny kid) with the teacher (the old cow).

4. What are the differences between day and night? Write the differences. Divide a paper in half. Label the top of one side *Day* and the top of the other side *Night*. Draw pictures to describe what you do during the day and at night.

5. Research and classify nocturnal and daylight animals. How are they alike?

6. Design and create a scarecrow that you would like to have for a friend.

7. Design a new pair of socks that you would like to wear.

8. Write a paragraph that tells what you do when you cannot sleep at night.

Activities for Other Bill Martin, Jr. Books *(cont.)*

Chicka Chicka Boom Boom

Authors: Bill Martin, Jr. and John Archambault
Illustrator: Lois Ehlert
Publisher: Simon and Schuster, Inc., 1989

1. On a large drawing of a coconut tree, write the 26 capital letters of the alphabet. On a small drawing of a coconut tree, write the 26 lowercase letters of the alphabet.
2. List the letters of the alphabet that rhyme with tree: B, C, D, E, G, P, T, V, and Z. Then write a new rhyme about an alphabet tree and these nine letters. Example: A and B went looking for an alphabet tree and took along their friends, C and D.
3. Create math word problems using the letters in the story. Example: A, B, and C were at the top of the coconut tree. Then D, E, F, and G climbed up the tree. How many letters were there in all?

"Fire! Fire!" Said Mrs. McGuire

Authors: Bill Martin, Jr. and Richard Egielski
Illustrator: Richard Egielski
Publisher: Harcourt, Brace and Co., 1996

1. Review the careers of the women in the book. Then discuss a career you would like to pursue when you get older.
2. Visit a fire station or have a firefighter visit the class to discuss the career of being a firefighter.
3. Create a list and learn the emergency phone numbers in your town, city, etc.
4. Create a rhyme, using words that rhyme with the students' names in the class.
5. Read each page with pictures on it. Then predict what will happen on the continuing wordless pages.

The Ghost-Eye Tree

Authors: Bill Martin, Jr. and John Archambault
Illustrator: Ted Rand
Publisher: Henry Holt and Co., 1985

1. Write a story about a time you were afraid of something. Be sure to include a setting, the characters, the problem, and how you solved the problem.
2. Plan a Class Hat Day. Everyone brings a favorite cap or hat to share with the other students. Draw pictures of the favorite hats and caps to display on a bulletin board.
3. Read the book to the class and have the children expressively read together the words in italics.
4. Follow the various appearances of the black cat throughout the book, and discuss the significance of its character in the story and why it appeared throughout the milk-run and milk-errand escape.

Activities for Other Bill Martin, Jr. Books *(cont.)*

The Happy Hippopotami

Author: Bill Martin, Jr.
Illustrator: Betsy Everitt
Publisher: Harcourt, Brace and Jovanovich, 1991

1. Design a pair of beach pajamas for a happy hippopotami.
2. Draw and color Popsicles shaped like fruit. Label them with prices of five cents to ten cents.
3. Research the history of different holidays around the world, including the May Day celebration and how it is observed.
4. The happy hippopotami did many things to make himself happy. Write a book about things that make you happy.
5. Create a list of how the word "hippopotamus" was changed in the book.
6. The hippos inspired each other because they had fun together and helped each other. Write about and share how you have inspired someone.

Here Are My Hands

Authors: Bill Martin, Jr. and John Archambault
Illustrator: Ted Rand
Publisher: Henry Hold and Co., 1987

1. Create individual, student-written books about the basic body parts, following the format in the book. Brainstorm the functions of each part, beginning with the head. Then follow a word pattern for each page. Example: Here is my head. It is for. . . .
2. List the verbs or action words with similar word endings which are used in the book.
3. Reread the book orally together and act out each body part function, as it is described.

Listen to the Rain

Authors: Bill Martin, Jr. and John A. Archambault
Illustrator: James Endicott
Publisher: Henry Holt and Co., 1988

1. Keep a weather journal for a week and use adjectives to describe the weather each day. (Example: a sunny day; gray clouds; bright, blue sky)
2. Review the meaning of rainbow. Draw and color a rainbow. Some say there is a pot of gold at the end of the rainbow. Write a story about what you would do with a pot of gold.
3. Describe your before and after feelings when listening to sounds or anything that can be heard. (Example: hall noise, classroom sounds, music, sirens, wind, etc.)
4. Pretend you are an insect, animal, or plant caught in the rain. What would you do? Then write about what you would do if you were caught in the rain.

Activities for Other Bill Martin, Jr. Books *(cont.)*

The Maestro Plays

Author: Bill Martin, Jr.
Illustrator: Vladimir Radunsky
Publisher: Henry Holt and Co., 1994

1. Discuss the meaning of adverbs and how an ending is sometimes added to verbs to make an adverb, such as: quick/quickly, slow/slowly, etc.

2. Brainstorm a list of verbs that can be changed to adverbs by adding *ly*. Then use one of the adverbs in a sentence and illustrate its meaning. Use different-sized letters. (Example: softly / **loudly**)

3. Create a list of verbs, and add *ingly* to form nonsense words such as: jumpingly, winkingly, etc. Say the words with rhythm, and draw pictures to illustrate the meanings of the new words.

4. List the musical instruments in the book in ABC order. Then define and categorize the instruments into groups of brass, string, and percussion instruments.

5. A *maestro* is a master in an art. Write a book about a maestro. Describe the three story parts: beginning, middle, and end. (Example of a beginning: The maestro plays proudly, loudly, etc.)

The Magic Pumpkin

Authors: Bill Martin, Jr. and John Archambault
Illustrator: Robert J. Lee
Publisher: Henry Holt and Co., 1989

1. If you had a magic pumpkin, what would you do with it? Write a story about it.

2. Cut different-sized pumpkins in half and then count their seeds. Graph the number of seeds. Then plant the seeds in peat pots and record their growth.

3. Give each child an original pumpkin. Paint a face with acrylic paint and spray with polyurethane spray to preserve. Draw a *before* and *after* picture of the pumpkin.

4. Discuss the words "turncoat" and "traitor." Create situations where a person could be defined as a traitor or a turncoat.

Activities for Other Bill Martin, Jr. Books *(cont.)*

Swish!

Authors: Bill Martin, Jr. and Michael Sampson
Illustrator: Michael Chesworth
Publisher: Henry Hold and Co., 1997

1. Review basic basketball rules and how points are scored. Play a game of basketball and keep the score.

2. List and discuss basketball words in the book: *referee, dribble, rim, rebound, basket, jump shot, time out, pass, steal, pivot*, etc.

3. Review how numbers are used in the story: on the scoreboard, on the uniforms, points for different baskets, one last play, etc. Create math word problems using these numbers. (Example: The Cardinals had 44 points. Cindi made a three-point basket. How many points are there now for the Cardinals?)

4. List the rhyming words in the book. Then add other words with similar word endings. Create original rhymes using these words.

5. Discuss and observe different logos for athletic teams. Then design logos for the Cardinals and the Blue Jays.

6. Create a Class Hall of Fame. Feature an asset of each child, along with a picture and display them on a bulletin board in the classroom.

The Wizard

Author: Bill Martin, Jr.
Illustrator: Alex Schafer
Publisher: Harcourt Brace and Company, 1994

1. Reread the story together and find familiar words that have been reversed, such as *I pong. I ping.* (ping-pong) and *I dong. I ding.* (ding-dong) Then discuss how the illustrator has expressed the words in pictures.

2. Compare and discuss the different meanings of the word *wizard* and other familiar uses of the word, such as *The Wizard of Oz*.

3. Have the students pretend they are wizards and then create a potion that could be used to solve a problem. Write stories about the potions and their importance.

4. Choose a character in the story to follow through the whole tale. Observe and record the character's actions on each page of the book.

5. List the verbs mentioned in the book. Then add other words with similar word endings. Create, write, and illustrate nonsense rhymes using these words.